T0128269

In DUE TIME

A Collection of Poems

LARRY GREEN

BALBOA.PRESS

A DIVISION OF HAY HOUSE

Balboa Press books may be ordered through booksellers or by contacting:

Balboa Press
A Division of Hay House
1663 Liberty Drive
Bloomington, IN 47403
www.balboapress.com
1 (877) 407-4847

Because of the dynamic nature of the Internet, any web addresses or
links contained in this book may have changed since publication and
may no longer be valid. The views expressed in this work are solely those
of the author and do not necessarily reflect the views of the publisher,
and the publisher hereby disclaims any responsibility for them.

The author of this book does not dispense medical advice or prescribe the use
of any technique as a form of treatment for physical, emotional, or medical
problems without the advice of a physician, either directly or indirectly. The
intent of the author is only to offer information of a general nature to help
you in your quest for emotional and spiritual well-being. In the event you use
any of the information in this book for yourself, which is your constitutional
right, the author and the publisher assume no responsibility for your actions.

Any people depicted in stock imagery provided by Getty Images are
models, and such images are being used for illustrative purposes only.
Certain stock imagery © Getty Images.

Print information available on the last page.

ISBN: 978-1-9822-3734-9 (sc)
ISBN: 978-1-9822-3735-6 (e)

Balboa Press rev. date: 10/18/2019

Contents

He's Always There

When I bow at His feet
And He gently strokes my hair
I enjoy a sweet retreat
withou a single care
'cause He's there
The world may be crumbling
with war and pestilence
but strength is in His shoulder
And when life makes no sense
He's there
just where
He needs for me to need for Him to be
so He
can bless my dreams
And hear the screams and sorrows
knowing all our tomorrows
as well as our yesterdays
yet He still seems to say
I love you still
I never will
not be there
to share
your screams from within
and I've always been

By Whom All Exists

How could it be
we've lived the time
cried the tears, smiled the grins,
wiped the tears, wiped off the chins.

We're seen so much, we've laughed
and cried
we've won
we've lost
we've tied
and yet
we're here once again on the brink of regret.

How long
endure
how measured
unsure

what cure
can be found
when the relationship
runs aground?

the only matter now
is taking each day
one step at a time
now matter the delay

the ship will come
there is no doubt
when it does our hearts
will jump and shout

we'll know our time
on earth is done
and we shall see
the crowns we've won

Polished, radiant, brilliant
no less
we'll cast them at the feet
of the VERY BEST

At Jesus feet,
our achievements glow
He it is that gives us
what we know
Let the praise be His alone
For whom all exist
and by whom all exist
and without Him
nothing exists

Bumpy (P)ride

Don't bother trying to respond
Things couldn't get much worse
We lived our fantasy before
In love we've been immersed

The ride's been sweet
I'm not surprised
the bumps have
knocked us off

We've been to this place before
It's always been this rough

At first I wondered if
I was blind to what was true
I didn't want to believe
It wouldn't work with you

No matter how I try
To bend, compromise, comply
I'm still at fault
I'm to blame
Things haven't changed
They're still the same

I refuse to believe
it can't work with you

I still love.......you.

Bending the Mind

I wondered why I gave my mind
to notions such as these
that only seem to destroy and hate
and give my mind a squeeze

why are there such as bend the mind
a man might ponder through
the pain of such a desperate cry
that's sad for me and you

our histories mesh like a poor man's cry
a wailing never heard
the soul is crushed by the green monster's lust
and guilty souls occurred

how many more voices
from slain men's souls
and still the ladies pay,
we're not to blame when men play games
and tear their hearts away

we simply fail to accept our lot
In God's wondrous grace
His methods, tact, and eternal love
still baffle the human race

Looking Forward

you thought you were wiley
before the end of time
your influences and puffs of smoke
were nothing, if not sublime

but what has now, at this point been perceived,
though at the time was not believed
because you managed to deceive
the multitudes just trying to relieve

the misery and pain you caused
with subtlety and wile you kept the lost
dragging souls to the great abyss
always done...with a friendly kiss

you were crafty and subtle from Edenic times
but you've been revealed as times unwind
the truth's been told all along
and He now sings the Victor's song

the dust has cleared
tribulations past
many of us knew
what it would be...at the last

the King of Kings
our crowns cast at His feet
receives to His glory
all the praises that's meet

it was Jesus Christ from the garden
whose victory foretold
His heel shall bruise your head
We've heard written in His Word.

There's been no surprises
All were warned from the first
in the garden of Eden
when your deceiving lips pursed

your beauty and guile
has intrigued man since
for all of history, you've convinced
the evil you've quietly tempted
us to do...

your head's been crushed now
the truth's unfolded sure
many martyr's blood's been spilled
and Savior's even more

we've known by faith
long before time's end
because Jesus, in writing,
news of His birth, life, and
death and resurrection...
...did send

long before the end of time
long after the settling of dust
all during the span of man
the truth has been
revealed to us...
some accepted
some did not
but now, the truth is known
what's what is what

the saga near over
decisions made
the sunset of the past
long echoes of history...in the shade

Now eternity's bells forever
shall ring
whenever we like
a lark will sing

and we'll forever His glories declare
all the multitude of believers...
...we'll all be there.
we'll cast our trophies at His nail
pierced feet
and forever give Him the glory
that's meet

These Hearts of Ours

Ah these hearts of ours
how brittle when they're bent
and all the while we simply find
it's wasted time we've spent

what uncertainty this love
how fragile when it's flexed
as muscle taut or flowing dread
a shame the time it wrecks

egomaniacs with an inferiority complex
a famous man once said
and loneliness haunts him still
a monster never dead

must I really let it go
just so I can be?
In order to be normal
must I lose all sense of me?

dying to oneself each day
would not be bad unless
it's a stubborn refusal
of reality to address

and then there's that monster self
who rears his ugly head
surviving for him is real
he has the deathly dread

so each day that I awake
I'll awaken with a smile
knowing well with every step
I have another mile

what fills each moment of every day
let God decide my fate
until He brings it all about
I simply have to wait

The Worst Part

the worst part about being me
is floating about the worldly sea
wanderin', wondering, wallowing
in the mire
once on fire
then not
once cold
then hot.

the worst part about being me
is the confinement I'm in just to be free
locked in life,
lost in love
once a hawk
then a dove.

the part I like least about being me
is my stubborn unwillingness to walk with Thee.
trying out the reins
forgetting the blood stains
neglecting the dawn
acting as if I was my own.

this is how from self to flee
keeping one's heart and mind on Thee
for Thou wilt keep him in perfect peace

whose mind is stayed on Thee because he
trusteth
in Thee

the best part about being me
is when I most resemble Thee
rising above the worldly sea
imprisoned so I can be free
more willing now to talk with Thee
than when I wandered
in the mire
once on fire
then cold as ice
enticed by worldly lusts.

Sleeping Beauty or Live and Let Live

He heard her respiration
and listened for the next
he wondered why he loved her
when she had his soul so vexed

Tomorrow he'll be lonely
because she's not really there
to her it doesn't matter
she doesn't seem to care

lately she's so distant
he just can't figure why
she's easily distracted
the man sit's there and sighs

all his guts are churning
all his heart is scared
why did he begin this
why had he even dared

frightened as a child
he relives that awful pain
and every time he loves her
he lives through it all again

Time's supposed to be for healing
the scars stick out like sin
he worried where it was going
would she ever let him in

Caring is the daring
her past has scared her too
he thought to truly love her
was the best thing he could do

but true love isn't selfish
he's always there to give
otherwise she's walking
and it's back to live and let live

Sitting In the Dearth of Man

Tired, restless
lonely, forlorn,
wondering why I was ever born.

This no longer haunts
from a past so bleak
Restoring the joy
making strong from the weak.

What brought the change
'neath the stains of sin
man is but a man again
knowing of God, but refusing Him
choosing to wear the stain of sin.

Sitting in the dearth of man
wasting time with pen in hand
Hope to find the answers here
in quiet time, my soul to bare

the hope of life eternal springs
where rainbows shine, a robin sings
children laughing, no more dearth
upon the saddest joy on earth.

a darkened sky, a thunderous roar
to shake foundations through yon door
beginning back where time began
the darkening dearth upon the land

though full of peace and swept with joy
a happening beyond nature's ploy
hopeless yet with hope of mirth
to end this struggle of wallowing dearth

Life Goes By

I watch life go past my window
like the dust and leaves, the wind goes by
some friends, some strangers,
some make me wanna laugh,
some make me wanna cry

I wonder where they're going
I can't help look for why
these friends of mine, these strangers
we sit and laugh,
sometimes we cry

Looking through my transparent self
wrestling with my own inner spy
Time, like life,
I'm watching fly by

Destiny's the journey's fuel
Engulfed in this self-made duel
Time glides by
when I don't even try
sometimes I'm glad
I can't help wonder why
sometimes we all cry

Friends and foes
alike drift by
I'm left wondering
asking why

Sharing Souls

what you've done to me
is what I wanted done
this heart sought a place to love
it seems you are the one

you've let me share your soul
an oasis in the heat
what brought this miracle about
that you and I should meet?

What you've done to me
let's shout it from a cloud
let's rejoice and kick our heels
and shout it right out loud

Waiting On The Shelf

She told me being there
would invade her space
so I had to question
why she was kissing on my face

each one trying to steer
their fate by their own self
meanwhile let the other
simply wait upon the shelf

wait until the morrow
perhaps I'll love you then
I have not felt so exasperated
since I don't know when

what destiny's provided
as each sun goes up and down
the soul's grip is subsiding
should I smile, or should I frown

Song of Love

A leaf expressed it's wishes one day
to the sun and the earth and even to the soaring,
gliding, carefree birds;
To be shadowed would not do, but there must be heat and light,
and oh, so much love.

"Let me endure this day with moist, green freshness, please"
For you see, the leaf loved the sun.

Whether to carry away on a song that golden morning,
when all was singing the echoes of the steaming hill,
And though there perhaps be a danger
lying in wait for the unexpectedly in love.

Ah, but in love with the song, the trees, the flowing, chilly
ripples of a smooth wind

The wind was kind for it came at the finest time...
...glances exchanged an endless love letter
that told wonderful things
of romance and heart beats, and yes, even sweaty palms.
The quiet of a mellow stream whispered that there
is no such thing as time

Soar away with me, soar away and away and away
On to where the people always sing and never cry.
Let us go where a rainbow is king

and it's beauty can be bathed in
until that lonely time, (yes, there is time)
when the birds sleep and their song ceases
the stream cannot bring itself to trickle;
hopes and the sun browns the green moist leaf;
and love is gone

To Draw A Dream

To draw a dream
with pen of black
Take the universe apart
and forgot how
to put it back.

The strain draws life
from the furrowed souls
pecking down the ones
who proves the roles.

To see what wailed
from a distant shore
would beg for stardust
evermore.

What dreams would sing
discordant twangs
and wrestle till dawn
with crumbling birth pangs.

What dreams were they
that saw the sun
jubilant bliss
on the run.

The peace which drew
a breath from whence
no on else
could walk the fence
And keep the dream in firm suspense.

Where would the thought of tiny trains
originate in children's brains
the slurp of soup
the dread of death
would hope the monster
would lay to rest
Until the dream some horror brew
I dream the dream I never drew

Bleeding Heart

all my suspicions after all were true
I knew he would make further contact with you
for some reason you held on to his stuff
easy for you, to me it's been tough

you play with my heart
with such absence of mind
it seems to be cruel
of the wiliest kind

seems it doesn't matter
my feelings get hurt
when your past is now present
and you're so curt

when will it hit you
it matters your trend
and the very way
you look at other men

do I have your heart?
or am I your toy?
it ruins our laughter
it crumbles my joy

I knew it would happen
and now it has
a refreshing reminder
a fragrance of past

here I sit
wondering again
just when I thought
you were free from other men

since he's back in town
will he try again
you can't stop him
a man is a man

I appreciate
the fresh jealousy rage
you know I could write
page after page

this type inspiration
I don't really need
it stirs up ugly passion
and makes my heart bleed

Pageantry of Infidels

pageantry of infidels
rank and file through the glade
wasting through doubting trials
and what a waste is made

the worker
struggling
daily routine
wondering of what worth it's been

easing into the calm of day
when flashing lights go away
the stress, frustration
lingers long after the whistle blows
and the calm is betrayed

like a wanton child
clinging to the warmth
of apron cloth
on a hot summer day

exposed to the light, the heat,
until the doubting and wasting retreat
the trials bring new strength
and new swiftness to the feet
light the way
lifting up hands

strengthening for the
re-entering
from the glade
the rank and file
in the dark woods
with the endless
pageantry of infidels

Black Hole Soul

I went on a journey to the depth of my soul
and all I found there was a dark empty hole
And I thought to myself, 'This is no place to start,
The pit of my own deceitful and wretched heart
I begin my journey there, though it's where the search ends,
so I can be a better example for my loved ones, and friends.
I want to teach others to fear the Lord
and find the place where blessings are stored.

But I feel locked in to this dark black hole
where I breath in anguish like the dust of coal,
I've been here awhile, and I'm in here still,
I want to get out, but sometimes feel I
never will

Crossroads Musings

What words composed could affect the heart
giving birth to joy and peace in the inner part
Growing strong and deeply rooted as a burly oak
And wearing a robe of righteousness, though just a ragged cloak

What decisions made at crossroad's choice
when one discerns the still small voice?
Alternate routes delay the growth
Forsake temptation, let grace betroth

Time runs out, more swiftly each day
May we nourish our souls without delay
Keep our words pure and seasoned with salt
Rather than tongue-lash our neighbor and say "It's all his fault"

Earnestly seek the Way, Truth, and Life
Too many others are caught up with strife
At the end of the pathway, when all's said and done
Those who follow righteousness will have the battle won.

What words composed these sentiments?
If tried the results are eminent
They've withstood the test through the ages
And documented on history's pages

Doing Only My Very Best

What emptiness when rage is gone
a void is made, and so on;
a gentle vacuum begins to draw,
new life into the listless soul

put off, put on
always both
from destroy to create
endeavor to betroth

a soaring finds
the air to life
the heart, the spirit
to end the rift

reconcile
flowing peace
rest assured
soft as fleece

what else considered
when hatred ceased
all the fury had been
released

what was left when man stood alone
the spirit, the soul, the flesh, the bone

a beating pulse
blood for life
time to pause
rest from strife

let life have it's desired bliss
enjoy life, and that you exist
remember joy when playing young
and trying to make sure
every song is sung

I lost the sea
the tempestuous sea
that used to rage
inside of me

the crashing roar
the thundering awe
was swept away
like I never saw

as if the wind obeyed His will
and when I sinned
though I said I never will

soon enough He knew the very place
where I would end up
being lost in space
never to set foot on land again
I might as well have been judged insane

Oh, so true I'll never be
as perfect as I want to be
I'm forever sentenced, I guess
destined to just do my very best!

am I just here to fill the space
that would be if I weren't
to mingle with the ashes
once the element is burnt?

a rudimentary article
exasperatingly
delivering a message
long lost upon the sea?

what has been said
then would one inquire
having lost that vain desire
pleasingly quieted amidst the storm

at twilight's hour
darkness come on
no more light
until dawn

once again the blooming rose
continues eliciting calm repose
life's worthy cause
restored to light
rejoicing the life can still ignite
exploding gently in the breeze of rest
to remember God knows you're doing
your very best

Evening Song

evening sang a quiet song
that seemed to last the whole night long
a peaceful dream of floating wings
soaring gracefully where angels sing

whispers whispered when dawn slipped in
while entered soon the new day's din
we worked then played, then rested till
a quiet song the evening filled.

Reborn

Weathering the awful tempest
struggling, pushing, ever onward
forward to the seemingly gray shroud goal
soon it will be more apparent
how valuable the human soul

returning laughter in the heart
removes the burning, aching pangs
the thrusting, biting, angry gallows
convincing man where destiny hangs

restoration ever offered
some accept and others scorn
man refuses to acknowledge
the magnificence of one reborn.

Almost A Beautiful Day

Troubled days are ended
the streams o'er flow with grace
The time has come, when sorrows mended
Triumphant calls echo
throughout the human race

In a vast and awakening cloud of peace
the blossom of a fresh hallowed song
rings forth the tidings that war has ceased
and it now it's time to right the wrongs.

Enveloped in a capsuled world
beckoning await the call
The problems that once kept the world in peril
are not relevant at all

Restore the beauty and love and charm
the spring where birds do soar and sing
Ne'er again shall the earth be alarmed
by the death and fear that war doth bring

And all these hopes shall never be
the dreams go up in flames
these promises we'll never see
and only man is to blame

Lobotomy of Love

a man lobotomized by love
what torment, grief, and pain
and yet when he's done healing
he starts it all again

I find the problem common
many men have cried
and if they said it wasn't their fault
I'm here to say they lied

We each must hold our own
learn not to give away
our heart which gives us light and love
and tells us when to stay

A woman's love is fleeting
like the wind it comes and goes
and they always leave you crying
why? nobody knows

Caring People Caring

Caring people caring
healing of the ill
smiling and cheering
time to take our pills

so we can get better
and live our lives again
get back in the street
and live with our fellow man.

Caring people caring
protecting from the dread,
the fears and the scaring;
we come here to be fed.

The staff here nurtures and encourages
so we can find our selves
they don't treat us like were objects
sitting on the shelves

but human beings with problems
which need to find a cure
but it's the caring people caring
which makes the healing sure.

the staff here makes the difference
because they are people too
and they know what it's like
when things aren't going right for you

promoting growth
and strength and courage
moving on and pushing forth
it's caring people caring
behind the healing force

helping sort life out
rejoicing when we heal
asking us each day
just exactly how we feel

the people here are caring
that show through their smiles
it pours through their every act
of going the extra mile

I wonder if they know
just how much they mean
if they know the difference they do make
in the patient's whole life scene

I just wanted to jot down
a few thought I felt like sharing
to express my gratitude
for all you caring people caring

What Folly Toward Mental Health

what folly is this
called treatment toward health
that everyone knows
simply drains the state's wealth

the state hospital is when
certain criminals are treated
no way justified
so the argument's heated

dangers presented
to individuals and staff
when it's all said and done
only evil has the last laugh

"Walking Toward the Food"

walking toward the food
like every other morn
a lifer, a stoolie
one was Mohawk shorn

routine had it's droning bore
often one could take no more
often lost sight of what it's for
this institute for the spirit-poor

from time to time
it's bearable
one of the broken seems
repairable

hope is had for what might be
can I help someone who might have
less fortune than me?

am I to forget
the human part?
ignore the urging
of my own poor heart?

am I trying to do
the impossible?
I ponder while gazing
through the window still

how to reconcile
these two thoughts
if not compassion
then here for nought

and then I remember
the victim's plea
crying out
what about me?

the heinous crimes
the past still holds
time spent here
justice upholds

the fat get fatter
as the days go by
a murder, a rape,
a little white lie

what really matters
as the time goes by?
is the reciprocate of
an eye for an eye

perhaps after all
the die is cast
the last shall be first
and the first, last

the gulf is fixed
but the door's not shut
trying to discern
just what is what

there is a truth
we all must face
the possibility
of disgrace

to speak the truth
not a myth
communicate the same
and yet more...herewith

at the end of this
and time is done
how will He judge
the battle won?

can I know now
what has to be?
the biker, stoolie, mohawk shorn,
and me?

obey all laws
don't break rules
the simple pass on
so do the fool's

the system is lame
and doesn't work
the meetings and memos
the catcalls and smirks

respect is an illusion
integrity's past
the values we share
are crumbled fast

a spirit looms
in these brightly-painted halls
it crushes the soul
when depression falls

failure's pending
or so it seems
when policy and procedure
squelches dreams

a fantasy of therapy
a figure-head
a front-for-funds
for the spirit-dead

bureaucrats and pride-wasted lame
repeating the error
(missing the point)
to judge what's fair

what must happen
is to look our best
nobody really cares about
the rest

as long as there's a way to get it off
our chest
how much has been given to 'invest'

unimaginable frustration
the only approach
in the entire nation

what works to reach
the desperate men?
before it's too late
and what then?

Original

Why? because every time I try a thought
I find it's been taken
my cry for originality therefore
I fear is therefore taken

motivation eludes me
during dreary times
joy escapes, sorrow climbs
and I go out of my mind

The Question

what is it that a man can write
about relationships
I have no sage advice to give
can't think of clever quips

Two separate souls entwined
simple, yet it seems
One has the other's heart
and one has shattered dreams

Loneliness engulfs the mind
fear of such remains
a man will tear it down to find the truth
regardless of the gains

Communication, truth, and love
ingredients the same
when all the fighting rage is o'er
who knows what remains

Pondering War

Scratching and scrawling
in cement pond's bottom
between those hills
from where comes my help
toward the mid-line
with flurried thoughts
during Spring's late rain
spattering the parking lot
a reflective time
while cleansing occurs
our little town's favorite breakfast spot
idle chit-chat and gossipy slurs
at war's bitter end
and sorting yet to do
feeling proud of being
of the red, white, and blue
the death toll's shadow
darken's the joy
not all lovers will see their soldier boy
those fathers and sons
though the battles have been won
will miss the coming home
to family's open arms
traded their life
for family, factory, and farms....

Another gust and spattering still
musing through life's window sill
where's everyone going?
Where have they been?
They've done it before
they're doing it again
who knows the beginning from the end?
I wanted to write you
while the Spring winds gust
while clearing some cobwebs and
washing out some dust
While my life is changing
while life goes by
I want you to know
what's on my heart and mind

Joy and Sorrow

may it never be said of me
a single day was spent in vain
for once I've closed my eyes tonight
I hope to open them again

life is full of joy and love
and life has pain and sorrow
I hope you've seen the good today
and see more good tomorrow

each day is a gift from God
let's fill each one with peace
let sorrow have but yesterday
today let love release

Loved but Lonely

I'm loved but lonely
a condition I own
I've had it forever
since before I was grown

there have been women
they come and they go
why this one would stay
I may never know

she sometimes seems attentive
and sometimes not there
sometimes she loves me
and yet doesn't care

she's not really able
to give her whole heart
but this information
I had from the start

The Drifter

The drifter launched from the curb this morning
and was suddenly out in traffic
without warning
Then he was back on the sidewalk
and smiled at the sky
while talking through his grin to a guy
who could not be seen with the eye

His old green army coat hadn't been washed in ages,
I wondered if he might have something contagious,
his conduct out in public was something outrageous,
I never saw him earning wages.

Someone said his family had money,
I thought to myself, 'Gee, that's rather funny'
He doesn't seem to have a dime to his name,
Isn't this an interesting twist to life's game?

What is it that one man's thinking is sound,
while another roams and wanders all over town?
each in their pursuit of happiness,
one clean-cut, the other a mess.

What determines what a man is on this journey,
Why is he a bum, and he's an attorney?
Is it simply the choices we make,
or did the one and not the other get a fair shake?

So many questions the mind tends to ponder
and pity for the one who seems destined to wander.
I hope he's able to stay warm at night,
Then I wonder if my concern is right.

Should I even care what happens to him?
Everyone has the same chance; it's all sink or swim.
Life seems to be so heartless at times;
the innocent suffer, the guilty get away with crimes

The irony, I guess, is remembering too;
that could be me,
or that could be you.

Tree Planting

let's plant a tree the couple said
then let's watch it grow
how high, how full, how beautiful
how tall we still don't know

nutrition, nurture, water, weed
sunshine, love and care
shall from intense heat and sun
to block it's awful glare

a beautiful symbol of two in love
whose dreams were shattered oft
a place where birds of lovely songs
can find a place to loft
still whispering, though soft

let the earth give forth her song
may it stand for you and me
in 30 blessed years from now
we'll kiss beneath our tree

Dirty Dishes

Dirty dishes last forever
stacked so high in yonder sink
washing them would be much better
than letting the food on them rot and stink!

"I'll do them later," I usually say,
"I've something greater to accomplish today."

So there they sit in all their glory
wanting to be wiped in soapy water that's hot
the saddest part of my dirty dishes story
is that I usually don't care if they get done or not

It's no big deal, I realize that;
I'm not so sure it e'en need be said;
But before I put on the dishwasher's hat,
The idea must first sink into my head.

Just do 'em, darn it, you'll be glad you did,
which I always am;
But I look at the pile and begin my woes,
'cause now they're caked with dried eggs and ham!

The dirty dishes last forever.
I guess washing them, after all, is my fate.
On the other hand, I could get real clever,
and decide next time to use paper plates.

Sunbathing at Newport

The yellow flag flapped in the burning wind
Next to it another flag, also yellow, but with a black ball
The sun directly overhead listened as the
radios blared, the volleyball flew
and the people chattered.

The blue, wet, moving carpet held
White sails that guarded the
busy brown heavily toweled sand.
Birds flew around peeking at the
sun bathers

A helicopter inspected the grounds
while a man inspects his garden;
to see if anything was growing,
or what has died

For the sun, ever so hot and unkind
was disturbed by the confusion when
he was about to leave;
the streaming, rolling metal cluttered
the once beautiful country;
And children were heard crying.

A mackerel questioned the King about the
yearly invasion of their domain
but the King only frowned.
In the chambers the judge only uttered in a
quiet desperation, "Tourist go home!"

Growing Old

I sit there in the twilight hours
when men of old would light the fires
my light was long blown cold
as my twisted mind and body betrayed
I'd grown old

Farewell to Father

He would have been 58 today
but yesterday he passed away
On Easter morn he went home
And now we feel so alone
Our dear old friend is gone now
Where'd the years go; they went by so fast;
I don't see how

I used to stand by his shoulder when he drove the car
As a little boy you can't see very far, sitting down;
and we would clown around, him and me;
we were what you would call real close, you see;
Even time itself could not pull us apart,
His door was always open, as was the door to his heart

I love this man, we'll cherish his memory;
the time we had will always be with me.
We laughed, we cried; he was quite a guy.
I wish he didn't have to die
before I could tell him one more time,
I love you dad,
Good-bye.

A Father's Plea

Slow down, my son.
Reset thy pace.
Let me wipe that tear drop
from your face.

Give me the pain.
I'll take it instead;
if I can remove
those tears you shed.

Is there sadness, my beloved?
Do I detect grief?
Are you really okay?
Is it just my belief?

Where are you headed?
I frequently ponder.
Do you dream of that land
way up yonder?

Of all that I've taught you,
if nothing else,
be considerate of others,
and not only yourself.

Letter To My Kids

I set the keyboard out of the way
put it above the blotter
took out a piece of paper and pen
to write a letter to my sons and daughter

Joshua, Daniel, Bethany
my loves, my blood, my life,
above all else I love you
regardless the toils and strife.

I may not be a lot of things
there's many that I am
after all is said and done
after all, I'm just a man

I've failed, I've tried
I've only wanted the best
for you and your children's children's children
forget about all the rest

Ours has not been an easy course
it's just not been that way
let us give thanks to God
for each and every day

He never promised
the sun will always shine
or things would e'er
run smooth
but that He'd never leave
or forsake us
with Him we cannot lose

our lives are hard
there's misery and pain
with periods of good
then heartache again

it seems as though
we'll be overwhelmed
'til we remember
Who's at the helm

I'm thankful that
He knows the way
and has promised we'll be there
in that coming day

I wanted this to be
a letter of encouragement and uplifting
I don't want my family
left wandering and drifting

the best wisdom and advice
I leave with you this day
give your lives to Jesus
every ounce, every way

the rest is only confusion
the rest is shallow and damp
with Him there's life and freedom
and light from the Eternal lamp

men are men
and kill each other
we blame, we strike
we fight
brother against brother
father against son...
all in the name of what's right

but soon the shadows all will fade
and faith will be turned to sight
we will ride in glory
with Him who is called the Life

it will be the end of toil and strife
then there will be no sorrow
'til then we wait

in the pain we're in
and hope upon the 'morrow

the emptiness that now invades
the truth that life can hurt
will soon be turned to joyfulness
and praise our hearts exert

love will reign
time always tells
we know well
where Jesus dwells

this isn't theory
but solid truth
our faith is our solid
doubt blocking proof

my prayer as you know
has been for many years
'let us walk in a way that's pleasing to Him
regardless of the bitterness and tears

let the light shine
hide your life not under a basket
it comes much too soon
we end up in the casket

the reality is
my joy in you is so real
your mother and you three
are why I feel

you are everything to me
after God it's understood
you're all the best thing that's ever happened to me
you are everything that's good

I firmly believe with all my heart
our lives won't be for naught
Our God would not forsake us
For it is Him we've sought

We have truly searched His heart
We've wanted what He wants
Our flesh, the world, the devil
have fostered deviance

I only hope you all will learn
and walk better than me
let's show the Lord that sooner or later
He can rely on our family

as a youngster myself
when my parents divorced

a shock was delivered
and a decision was forced

which parent will you live with
which one will you leave behind
I know this may be harsh
I realize it may be unkind

I know this decision's important
but I really gotta know
the judge is gettin' restless
and everyone's gotta go

I realize you're only six
it isn't the best age we could've picked
if you could choose in a minute or two
which parent you'll live with, we've got paperwork to do

my children, I know
you've heard all this before
I just don't want you to go through it
please don't let it happen anymore....

this letter of encouragement
is meant to let you know
no matter what may come our way
it's allowed for us to grow

He would not let
a single tear
to trickle down our face
unless it was the same
for all the human race

He loves the world
e'en unto death
the greatest of all gifts
please give Him every breath
return to Him if you drift

Too Hot!

I love the heat
it's really neat
it makes me not really
wanna eat
I love the heat
it's makes me see
things apart
from reality
I hallucinate
when it gets so hot
it doesn't matter
if it's real
or not
When it gets this hot
I sweat and smolder
I wish I was in a place
that was colder
I love the heat
like passion

like love
it broils down on it's
members
from high above
The heat is cool
forgive the pun
when it gets this hot

like ten feet from the sun
I'm the one
who sweats and breathes deep
and looks for shade and a place to sleep
I'm headed for the beach
that's not a reach
get a tan
like a he-man
on muscle beach....
It's too stinkin' hot
like it or not
it's here for days
boiling hot rays
what's the diff...??!!
it's summer comin' on
load up the VW bus....
I'm gone.....!!!!

Valentine

Flowers and hearts
Blooming and pounding
Love looms in the air
Soft dreams whisper sounding

Petals of passion
As two persons unite
Caressing skin, oh yes
And souls knit tight

Dream on, my fair one
Rise up and come away
Let my love encompass thee
On this Valentine's day!

Black Sheep

I am the black sheep
having wandered from the fold
looking for the wind break
seeking shelter from the cold

evening has been long spent
the night is far gone
hoping for tomorrow
gathering strength from morning sun

future yields it's bright gleam
though a black sheep and rejected
finding refuge in the Shepherd
in His care and ne'er neglected

lonely, simply and so saddened
knowing pain, regret and grief
sharing such with One so perfect
though slaughtered with a common thief

The Journey's End

I realize the journey's end
may include what tomorrow sends
except, of course, that's not to say
the journey's end may be today

what e'er may be
I surely know not
Again I begin
at this very spot

I only know
what else may be
all must be part
of the plan for me

The journey's end
need not bring fear
well knowing though
it's time draws near

when I reach home
on yonder shore
I'll then know peace
forevermore

The Computer's Day

(Oh what a tangled web)

The internet
has caught my eye
the way it goes
is super high

Communicate
at the speed of light
can I talk that fast?
could that be right?

Around the world
in seconds flat
and back again
how is that?

There's just no end
to what one can see
stocks, news, people,
pornography

It's all there
no denying that
you can get there faster
than you know where you're at

A crossword puzzle
a weather report
a golfing game
what fun, what sport

It's addicting, I like it
I can't seem to stop
surfing all over
from spot to spot

It's grown on me, I'm hooked
I'm stuck there for good
spending way more time
than I should

I do business, entertainment
correspondence, no surprise
I even go there
to socialize!

Confound it, let's face it
the web's here to stay
it's what's coming up
more and more each day

Get used to it now
you might as well
it's the light bulb, the toaster,
it's convenient as...

Listen to this
Let's put it this way
it's sliced bread and the microwave
it's the computer's day

For People Who Don't Like Long Poems

When there is no one around to love
Remember you are loved
And if you were the only one who was
The Lord would still do what He does

If you were to be the only one who is
He would have still done what He did
'cause that's the way He is

Sport

Multi-millionaire athletes
entertain us on court and field
frankly, I'm shocked to admit
the power and influence they wield

role models for our children
endorse at us night and day
and we with itching ears can't wait
to hear what they have to say

can't wait to watch 'em play
to sell us night and day
and for such sums of pay
to while our time away

Unfinished Poem

...And so the seed began to tremble,
All the moisture soaked the life
Cracking, rocking
peaceful strife

But what, the seed
was of what new plant
or tree, or from some
form of life, I'd grant

no newness would apt burst forth
from such a grub as this
until the scorching heat
and the evening mist
regaining each new leaf
as the seasons passed
which ones would dry up and die?
which ones would last?

Empty promises,
never filled
Dreams which never came true,
though one was thrilled
to even carry the tone
of love for a time
for two in love,
was it such a crime?

that one should die
because of that
is beyond my understanding
the carrying the heart
the tears and smiles
and ne'er two lovers landing
on their own two feet
at least till she
began to drift away
from he
and the trembling seed
no longer shook
in fear and hiding
for the love of one
belongs seated in the heart, abiding

Not just the thrill, the fancy;
nor even for a moment's time
at least the continuous same
relates least to that of a crime

But when love dies, if that were true
It resurrects each time in my heart for thee
I really wish it were the same
for you

though the fury waits
as a grazing horse
through time the fate
would grow even worse

Softly waiting for each new dawn;
would each new seed which has been spawned
forget the seed which would die
before it grew numerous feet high
into a golden or a dying gray sky?

Why, one asks why
why in an eternity
escape the draw of paternity
or maternity for all
eternity

The seed, of course, would not be planted
because the sower did not want to be taken
for granted.
Would you do this?
Or course, my love.
Would you do that?
Of course, my love.
Esteem me gone with each new dawn.

Let Us Hear the Conclusion Then

trying to put the apple back
back where it belongs
men have written about it for years
it's always been in songs

how do we each find peace
in such a world as this
when men are killing men again
so they can find their eternal bliss

scruples are all turned around
all of us are scarred
when each of us have known all along
the human race is marred

does she love me, does she not
how many petals pulled
and now the question once again
you grasped and played the fool

but greater things demand our sight
and keep us entertained
it's too bad we lost our fight
drawn in the sand again

Printed in the United States
By Bookmasters